This Week...

WEEK OF / /

MONDAY

TUESDAY

WEDNESDAY

THURSDAY

FRIDAY

WEEKEND

Top 3 things to do

- [ ] ....
- [ ] ....
- [ ] ....

Notes

This Week...

WEEK OF __/__/__

MONDAY

TUESDAY

WEDNESDAY

THURSDAY

FRIDAY

WEEKEND

Top 3 things to do
- ☐ ....
- ☐ ....
- ☐ ....

Notes

This Week...

WEEK OF / /

MONDAY

TUESDAY

WEDNESDAY

THURSDAY

FRIDAY

WEEKEND

Top 3 things to do

- [ ] ....
- [ ] ....
- [ ] ....

Notes

This Week...

WEEK OF / /

MONDAY

TUESDAY

WEDNESDAY

THURSDAY

FRIDAY

WEEKEND

Top 3 things to do
- [ ] ....
- [ ] ....
- [ ] ....

Notes

This Week...

WEEK OF / /

MONDAY

TUESDAY

WEDNESDAY

THURSDAY

FRIDAY

WEEKEND

Top 3 things to do
- [ ] ....
- [ ] ....
- [ ] ....

Notes

This Week...

WEEK OF __/__/__

MONDAY

TUESDAY

WEDNESDAY

THURSDAY

FRIDAY

WEEKEND

Top 3 things to do
- [ ] ....
- [ ] ....
- [ ] ....

Notes

This Week...

WEEK OF __ / __ / __

MONDAY

TUESDAY

WEDNESDAY

THURSDAY

FRIDAY

WEEKEND

Top 3 things to do
- [ ] ....
- [ ] ....
- [ ] ....

Notes

This Week...

WEEK OF __/__/__

MONDAY

TUESDAY

WEDNESDAY

THURSDAY

FRIDAY

WEEKEND

Top 3 things to do

- [ ] ....
- [ ] ....
- [ ] ....

Notes

This Week...

WEEK OF / /

MONDAY

TUESDAY

WEDNESDAY

THURSDAY

FRIDAY

WEEKEND

Top 3 things to do
- [ ] ....
- [ ] ....
- [ ] ....

Notes

This Week...

WEEK OF / /

MONDAY

TUESDAY

WEDNESDAY

THURSDAY

FRIDAY

WEEKEND

Top 3 things to do
- [ ] ....
- [ ] ....
- [ ] ....

Notes

This Week...

WEEK OF / /

MONDAY

TUESDAY

WEDNESDAY

THURSDAY

FRIDAY

WEEKEND

Top 3 things to do

- [ ] ....
- [ ] ....
- [ ] ....

Notes

This Week...

WEEK OF / /

MONDAY

TUESDAY

WEDNESDAY

THURSDAY

FRIDAY

WEEKEND

Top 3 things to do

- [ ] ....
- [ ] ....
- [ ] ....

Notes

This Week...

WEEK OF __/__/__

MONDAY

TUESDAY

WEDNESDAY

THURSDAY

FRIDAY

WEEKEND

Top 3 things to do
- [ ] ....
- [ ] ....
- [ ] ....

Notes

This Week...

WEEK OF / /

MONDAY

TUESDAY

WEDNESDAY

THURSDAY

FRIDAY

WEEKEND

Top 3 things to do
- [ ] ....
- [ ] ....
- [ ] ....

Notes

This Week...

WEEK OF __/__/__

MONDAY

TUESDAY

WEDNESDAY

THURSDAY

FRIDAY

WEEKEND

Top 3 things to do

- ☐ ....
- ☐ ....
- ☐ ....

Notes

This Week...

WEEK OF / /

MONDAY

TUESDAY

WEDNESDAY

THURSDAY

FRIDAY

WEEKEND

Top 3 things to do

- [ ] ....
- [ ] ....
- [ ] ....

Notes

This Week...

WEEK OF __ / __ / __

MONDAY

TUESDAY

WEDNESDAY

THURSDAY

FRIDAY

WEEKEND

Top 3 things to do
- [ ] ....
- [ ] ....
- [ ] ....

Notes

This Week...

WEEK OF / /

MONDAY

TUESDAY

WEDNESDAY

THURSDAY

FRIDAY

WEEKEND

Top 3 things to do

- [ ] ....
- [ ] ....
- [ ] ....

Notes

This Week...

WEEK OF __/__/__

MONDAY

TUESDAY

WEDNESDAY

THURSDAY

FRIDAY

WEEKEND

Top 3 things to do

- [ ] ....
- [ ] ....
- [ ] ....

Notes

This Week...

WEEK OF __/__/__

MONDAY

TUESDAY

WEDNESDAY

THURSDAY

FRIDAY

WEEKEND

Top 3 things to do
- [ ] ....
- [ ] ....
- [ ] ....

Notes

This Week...

WEEK OF __/__/__

MONDAY

TUESDAY

WEDNESDAY

THURSDAY

FRIDAY

WEEKEND

Top 3 things to do
- [ ] ....
- [ ] ....
- [ ] ....

Notes

This Week...

WEEK OF / /

MONDAY

TUESDAY

WEDNESDAY

THURSDAY

FRIDAY

WEEKEND

Top 3 things to do
- [ ] ....
- [ ] ....
- [ ] ....

Notes

This Week...

WEEK OF / /

MONDAY

TUESDAY

WEDNESDAY

THURSDAY

FRIDAY

WEEKEND

Top 3 things to do

- [ ] ....
- [ ] ....
- [ ] ....

Notes

This Week...

WEEK OF __/__/__

MONDAY

TUESDAY

WEDNESDAY

THURSDAY

FRIDAY

WEEKEND

Top 3 things to do

- [ ] ....
- [ ] ....
- [ ] ....

Notes

This Week...

WEEK OF __ / __ / __

MONDAY

TUESDAY

WEDNESDAY

THURSDAY

FRIDAY

WEEKEND

Top 3 things to do
- [ ] ....
- [ ] ....
- [ ] ....

Notes

This Week...

WEEK OF __/__/__

MONDAY

TUESDAY

WEDNESDAY

THURSDAY

FRIDAY

WEEKEND

Top 3 things to do
- [ ] ....
- [ ] ....
- [ ] ....

Notes

This Week...

WEEK OF / /

MONDAY

TUESDAY

WEDNESDAY

THURSDAY

FRIDAY

WEEKEND

Top 3 things to do

- [ ] ....
- [ ] ....
- [ ] ....

Notes

This Week...

WEEK OF __/__/__

MONDAY

TUESDAY

WEDNESDAY

THURSDAY

FRIDAY

WEEKEND

Top 3 things to do
- [ ] ....
- [ ] ....
- [ ] ....

Notes

This Week...

WEEK OF / /

MONDAY

TUESDAY

WEDNESDAY

THURSDAY

FRIDAY

WEEKEND

Top 3 things to do
- [ ] ....
- [ ] ....
- [ ] ....

Notes

This Week...

WEEK OF / /

MONDAY

TUESDAY

WEDNESDAY

THURSDAY

FRIDAY

WEEKEND

Top 3 things to do
- [ ] ....
- [ ] ....
- [ ] ....

Notes

This Week...

WEEK OF __/__/__

MONDAY

TUESDAY

WEDNESDAY

THURSDAY

FRIDAY

WEEKEND

Top 3 things to do
- [ ] ....
- [ ] ....
- [ ] ....

Notes

This Week...

WEEK OF ___/___/___

MONDAY

TUESDAY

WEDNESDAY

THURSDAY

FRIDAY

WEEKEND

Top 3 things to do
- [ ] ....
- [ ] ....
- [ ] ....

Notes

This Week...

WEEK OF / /

MONDAY

TUESDAY

WEDNESDAY

THURSDAY

FRIDAY

WEEKEND

Top 3 things to do

- [ ] ....
- [ ] ....
- [ ] ....

Notes

This Week...

WEEK OF / /

MONDAY

TUESDAY

WEDNESDAY

THURSDAY

FRIDAY

WEEKEND

Top 3 things to do
- [ ] ....
- [ ] ....
- [ ] ....

Notes

This Week...

WEEK OF __ / __ / __

MONDAY

TUESDAY

WEDNESDAY

THURSDAY

FRIDAY

WEEKEND

Top 3 things to do

- [ ] ....
- [ ] ....
- [ ] ....

Notes

This Week...

WEEK OF / /

MONDAY

TUESDAY

WEDNESDAY

THURSDAY

FRIDAY

WEEKEND

Top 3 things to do

- [ ] ....
- [ ] ....
- [ ] ....

Notes

This Week...

WEEK OF __/__/__

MONDAY

TUESDAY

WEDNESDAY

THURSDAY

FRIDAY

WEEKEND

Top 3 things to do

- [ ] ....
- [ ] ....
- [ ] ....

Notes

This Week...

WEEK OF ___/___/___

MONDAY

TUESDAY

WEDNESDAY

THURSDAY

FRIDAY

WEEKEND

Top 3 things to do
- [ ] ....
- [ ] ....
- [ ] ....

Notes

This Week...

WEEK OF __ / __ / __

MONDAY

TUESDAY

WEDNESDAY

THURSDAY

FRIDAY

WEEKEND

Top 3 things to do
- [ ] ....
- [ ] ....
- [ ] ....

Notes

This Week...

WEEK OF / /

MONDAY

TUESDAY

WEDNESDAY

THURSDAY

FRIDAY

WEEKEND

Top 3 things to do
- [ ] ....
- [ ] ....
- [ ] ....

Notes

This Week...

WEEK OF __/__/__

MONDAY

TUESDAY

WEDNESDAY

THURSDAY

FRIDAY

WEEKEND

Top 3 things to do
- [ ] ....
- [ ] ....
- [ ] ....

Notes

This Week...

WEEK OF __/__/__

MONDAY

TUESDAY

WEDNESDAY

THURSDAY

FRIDAY

WEEKEND

Top 3 things to do
- [ ] ....
- [ ] ....
- [ ] ....

Notes

This Week...

WEEK OF / /

MONDAY

TUESDAY

WEDNESDAY

THURSDAY

FRIDAY

WEEKEND

Top 3 things to do

- [ ] ....
- [ ] ....
- [ ] ....

Notes

This Week...

WEEK OF __/__/__

MONDAY

TUESDAY

WEDNESDAY

THURSDAY

FRIDAY

WEEKEND

Top 3 things to do

- [ ] ....
- [ ] ....
- [ ] ....

Notes

This Week...

WEEK OF __ / __ / __

MONDAY

TUESDAY

WEDNESDAY

THURSDAY

FRIDAY

WEEKEND

Top 3 things to do

- [ ] ....
- [ ] ....
- [ ] ....

Notes

This Week...

WEEK OF / /

MONDAY

TUESDAY

WEDNESDAY

THURSDAY

FRIDAY

WEEKEND

Top 3 things to do

- [ ] ....
- [ ] ....
- [ ] ....

Notes

This Week...

WEEK OF / /

MONDAY

TUESDAY

WEDNESDAY

THURSDAY

FRIDAY

WEEKEND

Top 3 things to do

- [ ] ....
- [ ] ....
- [ ] ....

Notes

This Week...

WEEK OF / /

MONDAY

TUESDAY

WEDNESDAY

THURSDAY

FRIDAY

WEEKEND

Top 3 things to do

- [ ] ....
- [ ] ....
- [ ] ....

Notes

This Week...

WEEK OF __/__/__

MONDAY

TUESDAY

WEDNESDAY

THURSDAY

FRIDAY

WEEKEND

Top 3 things to do
- [ ] ....
- [ ] ....
- [ ] ....

Notes

This Week...

WEEK OF __/__/__

MONDAY

TUESDAY

WEDNESDAY

THURSDAY

FRIDAY

WEEKEND

Top 3 things to do
- [ ] ....
- [ ] ....
- [ ] ....

Notes

www.ingramcontent.com/pod-product-compliance
Lightning Source LLC
Chambersburg PA
CBHW081157070526
44583CB00021B/2874